TERRENCE ARJOON

THE DISINHERITED

UGLY DUCKLING PRESSE

Praise for *The Disinherited*

"Like Nerval, Rimbaud, and bruno darío, Arjoon offers ampules of vivid elixir—tilty, surprising, lively, terminal, decadent, elegant, and, in their way, devotional—to the goddess, Poetry."

—Joyelle McSweeney, author of *Death Styles*

"Haunted by Nerval and making brilliant use of that possession, the magic-wielding Terrence Arjoon offers the delighted reader a series of precise dreamscapes that dance between the colloquial and the fabular. Level-headed yet moonstruck, these poems lodge in the neo-Romantic first person, but with stark, headstrong, Expressionist velocity... Reading *The Disinherited*, we thrill to the cropped outpourings of a timeless poetic instinct, without frills or simulations, except of the enrapturing kind... 'Once I fled paradise and tried to be beautiful,' Arjoon writes; marvelously he has succeeded in his quest."

—Wayne Koestenbaum

"Here we have the infamy and drama of translation laid bare. Drafts of Gérard de Nerval lie next to Arjoon's own indelible poetry. This sudden marriage reads like a haunted parisian bouquet that is lovingly losing its petals. *The Disinherited* invokes a state of total immersion/resurrection that both poets and translators speak of as idyllic."

—Cedar Sigo

"...Just as Nerval's speaker crosses the Acheron more than once, Arjoon goes back and forth between realms throughout *The Disinherited*, his own words and visions fusing inextricably with the dead's, suffusing them with light. The result: an exquisite chiaroscuro."

—Mónica de la Torre

First Edition, First Printing

ISBN: 978-1-946604-39-2
Library of Congress Control Number: 2025940354

Ugly Duckling Presse
The Old American Can Factory
232 3rd St., #E-303
Brooklyn, NY 11215
uglyducklingpresse.org

TERRENCE ARJOON

THE DISINHERITED

CONTENTS

"when in the sky he sees eclipses come…
when some familiar planet disappears."

—Guillaume de Lorris & Jean de Meun

"BLACK ELECTRIC STORM IS HERE"

—Bongo Jerry

"There are cinders there." "Cinders there are."

—Jacques Derrida

PREFACE

Gustave Doré's 1855 etching *La Rue de la Vieille Lanterne* depicts a man hanging from a lamppost, tongue lolling out. The back alley staircase is crudely etched, thick gouges in the wood, crude iron bars, curlicue shadows like some forgotten script, etched intaglio by a craftsman tracing Doré's pencil drawing on the wooden block. Above the hanged man is a choir of angels, extending infinitely backwards, set in motion by Death's trumpet. Doré did not etch or print his pieces, and believed the true works were the drawings they were based on, that "his drawings, alone, could bear witness to his work, which in a sense only existed 'unengraved' and could only be seen thus in its true intensity."[1]

The hanged man, born Gérard Labrunie, wrote under the name Gérard de Nerval. Friend to Victor Hugo, Théophile Gautier, and Alexandre Dumas, he translated Goethe's *Faust* into French, badly, but admirably, as well as Schiller, Klopstock, and others. He wrote several novellas, including *Aurélia and Sylvie*; a suite of poems, *The Chimeras* (adapted here in this book); profiles of socialists; and travelogues of his journeys to Egypt and Turkey. He was a sort of proto-Symbolist, in that he believed that everything might be a solution, if only it were

1. Philippe Kaenel, *Gustave Doré (1832–1883): Master of Imagination*, exh. cat., (Musée d'Orsay, 2014).

looked at from the right angle. Nerval was plagued with nervous episodes, immense solitude, fixations on women, and overwhelming friendships.

Nerval's work is under the pull of opposing forces: the silence of the dead and their pervasive letters and communiqués, community and isolation, love and loneliness, of itinerancy and home. Writing, for Nerval, is *unwriting*, every sentence to be undone or contradicted at some later point, after his death. Here, in *The Chimeras*, is a call to all the gods, Greek, Hindu, Christo-Judaic, to make sense of this mess—prayers tempered by anger and wistful confusion.

Amid the adaptations of Nerval in this book are my own poems, written over the past three or four years. I like to think that they come from a similar place, or meet Nerval somewhere across these couple hundred years; I, like everyone, am lost in the wilderness of this century.

By embracing these opposites, of love and isolation, of itinerancy and home, incongruous, all of them, Nerval attempts to move beyond them: "What Nerval ultimately seeks, then, is a redemption from the very narrative of redemption."[2] So I approach the seven *Chimera* poems chimerically, with honesty—and where they deviate from his text, I've done so with his notion in mind that, "Everything is alive, everything is in motion, everything corresponds; the magnetic rays that emanate from me or from others flow directly through the infinite chain of creation."[3] Like Doré's etchings, may Nerval's poems forever exist unengraved.

---

2. Gabriel Trop, "Mythological Indifference in Schelling and Nerval," *The Wordsworth Circle* 50, no. 1 (2025): 108-26, https://doi.org/10.1086/702586.
3. Gerard de Nerval, *Aurélia & other writings*, trans. Geoffrey Wagner, Robert Duncan, and Marc Lowenthal (Exact Change, 1996).

LOW TIDE

Once I fled paradise and tried to be beautiful.
When I left I laughed loudly, so that people in the world
might hear me—as I live on the far side of the river.
For a while I wrote down the name of every living thing I saw:
I read the rocks and their panegyrics,
I read the crickets, the dirt, snakeskins, crystal texts boned
and deloused. Pick up that flower from the table. What is it?
Wisteria? Lupine? You don't know.
There is in me now a wormlike moment.
This movement makes me sweat painting clowns
into the coral beneath my feet. This fossil reveals small flowers
when lifted breath-swollen from a long night on my own,
a fractured graze of light which renders, ultimately, as more
    martinis.
The astronomer ordered one dirty, or, he was from
Terlingua, but we agreed that there is no right time
for the clock to stop, only that it just happens.

MOTH LIGHT

Point by point the body renders new landscapes:
calls firm logics of its matrices.

Pelagic confusion it is or isn't
the same leopard which sings—

throat read us this sign,
I have been written. And

flashes from a tumble
weed, city of night, hiss.

Everywhere soils thawing so
becoming something else

to freeze within which
from blur into light, light

into confusion and moon-move.
It may repeat prudence

into blurred light-like
cosmic frame; sky to head.

HOW WE GOT OUR NAMES

Nothing ever happened to me
while I was awake.

This nothing, daily living, grounded
me in the loam of the estate.

This nothing was a beetle in me—
a beetle in fine lace embroidery.

We enlaced the world back then
in jasmine memories. The smell of

sweat mixed with the cold beads
on the stone lashed with jasmine-entombed

meshwork. In the mornings the columns
behind the graven gates would thin out,

from that fog which traced
downwards towards the sea.

Inside it was warm,
and our tunics hung loose,

so that we would have to
bat away certain flies,

drawn to the stick and
the smell. In mornings the bogs

would emit a cooling vapor, so
we would go down by the gates, certain

that the bogs were producing
the fog which led the columns seaward

for our own benefit. Thinking on it,
it was one bog interlaced with strands of

walkable land, interlaced with bushes
growing with five-petaled white flowers.

The flowers which were strewn over the path grew well
in warm weather, and due to the cold morning vapors oft

withered and fell, stinking
with their perfume.

This is why they called me Jasmine Stagnation.
However, because the enmeshed land was so

walkable we decided
there were eight bogs, not one.

Given that the bogs
were located perpendicular to the gates,

we had planted a row
of birch trees at a diagonal

to both the bogs and the gates,
their density protecting us from the eyes

of the columns which
after the morning fog lifted would

return to peer through the gates
at our loose tunics hanging as we

harvested the felled jasmine petals.
However, since we would only

venture down under cover of
the morning fog, the men

outside would slip letters
under the gate describing these visions,

written on birch bark scraped
from the top of the yellow birch close

to the estate walls. Under cover of fog
we would walk down to the furthest birch

to harvest our paper,
on which we would inscribe these

prayers, dreams, letters.
Although the birch trees grew well

with moisture, and received adequate sunlight,
they were often killed by beetles

called bronze birch borers. The others
would flick these beetles off

and crush them underfoot, or
we would find them under our tunics

inside, clinging to the beads of sweat
rippled and hidden by the fine lace,

but I would never crush them.
Their long iridescent bodies would glimmer

in the dull morning fog, flattening into
a chisel at their rear.

But I wouldn't touch them.
They would scuttle over the white jasmine

as I kneeled,
and I would call them by their name.

This is why they called me the Penitent Borer.
The men would dig up the birch with chisels

once the beetles killed them,
and after stripping the paper

we cut it up for firewood,
the fire of which made

the interior exceedingly hot. At midnight
I would venture out to the gate

to watch the columns
sleeping on the grass, their ingrown hairs

and balding heads shining
in the flicker of flying carapaces.

This is why they called me Midnight's Gate.
The graves we dug for the men

were often too small, gravediggers striking
for the width of it.

In the off-season,
and kept away by the columns

outside, their graves filled with grains
and many small samaras.

EL DESDICHADO

I am a shadow—a fool—an inconsolable
aqueduct prince in my metabolic tower:
my tired soul—my moth constellation it
carries my brown melancholic sun.

Dancing nights in tombs you consoled me,
giving me pursed lips in Populonia,
the flower that pleased my tainted heart
and the trellis where the vine and wisteria agreed.

Am I Nerval or Villon… Harris or Rodney?
My face is red again from kisses; invisible hearts.
I dreamed in the cave where the mermaid swims…

And twice I cross the Tigris
phasing in and out on Orpheus' lyre
of the soup of saints, and the cries of scorpions.

THE HOURS

The Cinnabar Kid shook the universe:
Isis, the sea, rose up from the couch,
made a gesture of disdain toward her sick husband,
and old brilliant love blew mollusk-green through her eyes:

"Do you see him, there, dying of perversion,
all the frames of the world passing through his guts,
attached to his swollen feet and his louche eyes.
My god; the volcano, red shivers!

The eagles pass overhead, and a new spirit overtakes me,
I play Sibelius for him…
oscillating between love and hermeticism."

She flees on a golden beetle,
the night sea reflected in its own image,
and all heaven's rays shining under her scarf.

THE CINNABAR KID

That the Cinnabar Kid was at it again is no joke; some image of him sitting at the window
Or going through it, I—the moon, it was, um, with thee conversing I forget all time.
With Thea in the pleasure loam at Taix arguing over the bill

And Eight-Bog Marie's office, nothing on the wall, cinnabar lacquerware on the credenza.
In the adjacent room, we had just watched Solvent's Moon, and I slept on the couch
Which was some reenactment of a disappearance at La Ripa

Of the Cinnabar Kid in Terlingua a column of dust
Looking forward to Noumena at the block party
It causes shaking

There was a sudden wind and fog that morning, and no one knew where he departed from
I was shaky inside but I was really at a party with
Doing helium in the studio

Singing a waltz in the key of helium

Painting solvent on each other so the Cinnabar Kid might've laughed
In that bituminous way he laughed
Because it's time to cut trees and carve

Lacquerware inserts show the Cinnabar Kid's flight path
Now I keep the grain-light lit in the grain-shaped cave
Reaching out obliquely about a stepped-on snake in a letter

I had tampered with a photo of a snake, in the past
My arm shook while lying in bed

The Cinnabar Kid had to go to work the next day

So now I guess I'll be up forever

Breaking dishes in the kitchen, just keep dropping them

Earthy matter; just don't break the cinnabar

At Hang Seng, blues, keep overdrafting

My tent, it was small, and little raining, and we painted mud
    on each other's faces

I heard the Cinnabar Kid fell out of an airplane in Idrija

Later married a bucket maker who had seen a saucer of light in
    the well

Thus enstrangement became a suitable solution

For image-making, full of angles

And I felt tattered, but not dry back at the house

Or get married in the basement of the paint-chipped silo

CUTTLEFISHING

Hair stained the color of mollusk ink.
While my father is in the hospital I wait around;
I stand outside the bodega.
He had been out catching cuttlefish:
"You catch them mornings, right off the
quay by the rock wall the morning black and
the whales singing off the horizon, spouting in the air.
Thread a herring on the line, hands slick with oil—
you know it's right when the float sinks."
Later we would chuck the cuttlebones as far as we could
to the screamers out back. The brown-black
pigment stains his fingers.
The tears streak the pigment
when I get down on the floor to write.

THE AIR-LOOM

The oil below kept us all from sleeping for years.
But now we walk still under the crab-woods
hand in hand, our bodies forming an annulus
at the end of the world—this love was a fluid venture
through which the Oko flowed.

Off the coast finch red kellies sway in the darkness,
light reflecting off dull steel. With this stuff
going on some of them don't go back to nature.
They just rot in fields, or in cars in the jungle.
They just sit there a long time.

When my uncle died my father wore
a red string on his left wrist for two years.
When I was laid up there in the house
I heard a song. Fat leopards lay by me;
I heard a leopard song in the belly night.

The oil that was hidden in houses
is now in fat leopards. I found
a whistle in the arapaima's belly.
I found my grandmother's ring
in the black caiman's jaws.

The arapaima's song told of flying air looms
pumping oil through rigs of tubing into the ground.
This ground we walk on sopped dreams up
so we could hear the leopard talk through
the crush of roughnecks in the moon pool.

The moon pool roughnecks told of the
goddess who turns you

into a pink lily if you touch the moon.
Spud date approaching they dig deep in
the brine pool.

But after all this, who can resist
a penitent dog leg? The rumor that cleft through

was that the season called for more bones,
more bones—and in the end they delivered.

MYRTLE

I'm thinking of you—I smell you, divine enchantress,
haltingly, dressing, eating brilliant mille-feuille.
Your forehead flooded with light from Orvieto,
black grapes mixed with your shining hair.

In your cup, too, I tasted your drunkenness,
and in the lightning flashing in your eyes
when at Bach's feet they caught me praying,
driving in your car, amused, a descendant of the astronomer.

I know why the bottom of the volcano reopened…
yesterday you touched it with your feet
and suddenly the sky was filled with ashes.

Since then your clay gods shattered by a
Normandy breeze, always,
under these laurel branches.
Find Hortense!

THE SECRET OF NERVAL

The door is the bee.
The bee is a stress position.
A stress position is a peach pit.
A peach pit is ambiguity.
Ambiguity is a matter of style.
Style is a stone.
Stone is a transparent body in my heart.
My heart is a flat-headed fungi.
Fungus is an hour.
An hour is a hole in the ground,
mottled I.
I is a drug.
The drug is the breath of the crab.
The crab is great happiness.
Happiness is wind blowing on the mountain.
The mountain is a cangue.
The cangue is engorged limestone.
Limestone is the stinger of a bee.
A stinger is an infinite being living on the moors of death.
Death is your bed.
Rendered animation.
Animation is a row of honeycombs.
A honeycomb is a fish-shaped island.
The island is a designer thyrsus.
The thyrsus is a law in the world.
The world is a formal inflorescence.
Inflorescence is an evening brain;
Ribbon grass pulled up by a laconic midwife.
A midwife is a monument.
A monument is a tail in the water.
Metabolic vehicle.

A vehicle is a tunic breaking across the face.
A tunic is the moon falling.
The moon is present at its birth.
Birth is the oxen's neck.
Grave lightning.
Lightning is a lifting belly.
A belly is an oracle.
An oracle is a dry bone.
A bone is a door.

THIS EARTH, THIS PASSAGE
(After Isamu Noguchi 5/24/24)

In the city to build this
        city, whose terraces are
the color of stars, roundness,

to be departed from, blown green
in the wind. This Earth is the name
        of my belly, full of pear juice, and cherry

compote, skin daubed, fingerprints from
        my love, to cover my body. Round, this passage,
this Earth, to bring her back to me, to cover
me once again.

Butterflies and Charlotte's sparrows, and mint,
nothing appears more likely than a return,
somewhere on the underside of this century,

to that city whose aqueducts poured caffé
corretto down the avenues of this earth, muddy;
almost browned, languorous, but now nothing
looks less likely, the green light limned
in the basalt passages of my life.

ARTEMIS

The end is back… still the first;
And it's always the only one—or the only time:
And you my love, you, are you the first or the last?

Are you the first and last lover?

The one who loved you from the desk;
The one I love alone who loves me still;
She's death—or dead… Delicious! Torment!
The rose she holds is The Trembling Rose.

A Venetian saint with fox hands,
Rose with a violet cry, my lantern flower:
Did you find what you were looking for in the desert?

White roses, tombs! You insult the gods:
Tombs phantoms white votives brutish sky:
—Abysmal saints and more saints than trees!

THE ASTRONOMER'S DREAM

He stuck me at the glam rock party, the astronomer, eyes
glittering.
Drunk off Brandy Alexanders;
I woke up with a warm knife in my belly—worried...
And I cried all night wondering so. I summon something.
I was a bathing beauty at the estate, fingers stuck up in me like
a spindle—
a syzygy of delight. I think of Pink Venus; they are "making
me" feel things.
Because back then I wanted to be a dancer—eye-bags, skin-
picking and tremulous,
locking that nervous shake into form.
Dancing with Eight-Bog in swamp water she leans down to kiss
a red oyster.
I kiss a soft gold bead, she hates that, because I was en pointe.
Something, answering, a voice in silver or far thigh.

Moving eastward the river was frozen solid so we swung pick-
axes
in the night out through me and extending from twigs and
branches into the nearby towns.
One half of the valley is making love
to the other. She leaves me at the river's edge.
I can smell mint, cinnamon, teeth.
Sleep comes like a burst testament, or a faulty citation.

It comes out of me, like a tree.
There is wind today my friend,
though you yell into canyons parading beside them
as if feelings were felt, or worse, found.

So you adopt a new name and so do I.
But you got some seawater
in your mouth, and it made you nauseous.
When you spit it up, everything's up: cornerstones, acorn caps,
the blood and electric shock of the last hundred years
breaking like a mosaic. I too am troubled by the lassos, and
I am always thinking I should get flowers, too late.
Being trapped in this lateness, and so, late to it,
bells demarcate the boundaries of my body.
When words fall, shapeless, like an almond; space grows quiet.

I am struck by the pale straw color of that rock.
So reaching, an appendage, a dogwood,
I stole a sparrow to send this to you—carnal wisps surrounding
    wheels
binding the sky. The sun craves this posture.
A house appears, and a complex of tensions within it.

Give me a minute to get used to this again: I have been a mud
    bank.
I have been an ox. I lived in the sun for years
but for now it is the season of lakes,
and the pole stars that panic once shown through.

In film
withering mulberries sense
cutting wind.

Wind
forest, dabbing
dew in the dark.

Whose flute
is this?

This mountain,
 it eats.

Come night
it swallows.

Swallow pine nuts.
Thick foliage
roofs.

Do not become
everything.
Gross
mineral patterns swell.

Swelling
knee; ankle.
I make money disappear.

I fit inside.
I merge with
smoke and mist.

Mists barque in thin lanes
from the mountains.
End
with clear notes.

Fig fresh flutes
who are never
naked
in moonlight.

THE SECRET OF NERVAL

I never slept
for a long time.
Too many people
were talking.
In Cairo, in Todi,
on the train,
the Cinnabar Kid, drones,
Eight-Bog Marie,
blue frogs, Aurelie,
Nerval, pottery shards,
mineral springs, Isis,
Charlotte, scorpions, lamps,
and I wrote through silence.
All my notebooks
left blank.

THE STONE FOREST
(After Lisa Robertson)

That if I stand under this pole star binary knoll I'll have courage
to know my face and the sand look different,
I was born under the sign "limping dog,"
in the distance the osprey has taken over the hawk stand—
it could be seen from the back.

That I do not know from whence the dream came—
eyes are to see and ears to hear,
I have never been down there but if the rocks aren't too wet,
"limping dog" can come along too.
there was a shimmer across the back of the sky reflected in
the body
of water between the train and the estate, filled up, filled up.

That in the terraced city I see the graffiti on the former
monoplex's exterior wall and imagine it is me,
I was in fact "Faded Frog."
the night is already quiet and I am bound in it,
the circumflex extension of that quiet was *image of snow*,
it is brief.
this is the life I had, a bank of trees of one's openness or doubt.

That the snap of release,
the voices,
the marbled tenor he gives us,
the stacks of paper,
a rheumatoid sentiment,

that a permitted glare skimmed via hoof tracks,
I ask for it all,

I would walk to the baseball field,
something was on fire,
I met him in a bar,
I was no longer his wife.

That I froth wearily from a green vase,
an upscale wrecked beach with a necrotic stain.
I cant gracefully in a rose chiffon noose,
the whole problem tastes like apricots,
I should have left a little earlier.

DAPHNE

Do you remember, DAPHNE, our romance
at the foot of the sycamore, or under white laurels,
or under olive trees, myrtles, or the trembling sun,
the song of love… always beginning again.

Do you remember the TEMPLE, with that courtyard,
and all the lemons you bit into?
And the cave, fatal to lunatics,
where the sleeping serpent hates forever.

They'll come back to these places they miss!
Time will bring them back to the way they used to be;
the earth baking a prophetic soufflé…

Meanwhile, the scribe with the sunken eyes
sleeps in Daphne's arms
—and nothing shakes the graven gates.

DRONE ACUPUNCTURE
(After Leslie Scalapino)

I woke early and went to shower

in the darkness and saw and heard the couple having
intercourse. The parts of their bodies that were normally
covered by clothes were those of leopards.

That attitude being so ponderous of which parts were those
of leopards and which were not. That attitude out of the
question, of what I consider and do not consider.
Consider, uh, slipping a shoe off under the table in the evening.
Consider the delicate marbling on the skin.
Consider the state of corsetry, of, yeah, consider untying those
bows.
When I am in bed sometimes
I notice the parts of my body covered by clothes are those of a
leopard's.
Consider genitals as oblative precursor of sound—
Consider gold beads in ears…

the sun waning in the mouths of the dead and almost dead
my dream-brother far away in Los Angeles now too,
and the baroque movement of the sun—
Baroque, the sun baroque?

Consider the crowded dreams of leopards.
The gold beads in my ears
produced blue beams of light at night, before I woke to shower,
and they pointed me to the Leopard's Moon.

In the painting she is wearing a coral necklace, glancing at
herself in the hand mirror. Her clothes are off, but she does
not share the parts of a leopard.

Can I, in connection, be secure in the thought that I too might
bear a human anatomy, that in my dreams I can wander the
city of the living and the dead:

a radiant fantasy of strawberry ices

whose pink Venetian pillars crumble in my human throat,
and marrons glacés which appear
on the steps on the night of the New Year.
Now mouths steaming mornings, the night-watchmen consider
their egress.

When I turn leopard holding
the porch pillar the
immobile hawthorns and rush-
reaching panicles in the slumber vase,
I turn leopard in low red light.
When the song reaches home you are dead.

When I turn leopard
we are caught in the sand, I inside you,
by he holding the conch.

When I turn leopard the dream becomes ordinary.

Given, when leopards see the slumber vase, things become real
on the stoop.
In the real light of day, dreams become real, or, unclassifiable
emotions.

When I woke as me, the streetcars were electrified. I walked
down the tunnel into the darkness.
When I turned leopard I sang a song of daybreak in the city of
the unborn.
In the city of the unborn I see the mountains in the distance;
they do not excite me.

Given my knowledge of the city it was to my surprise to
uncover this new area of the city, where the leopards live.
Though the trees curve down on Lovers Lane,
I now long for real things: I dig them out of the earth

and bring them to Leopard Village.
I bring a fig metal brooch, I bring a lyre flower. I bring the
Leopard's Song.

THE MISTLETOE BOUGH

Laughing in a ditch next to the astronomer
because I tricked him into adopting a mistletoe.
Clouds pass over and under, and through it,
and there was a jasmine shrub, which come spring
I would weave around my head telling stories
and talking forever only a stone's throw away from the
beginning of cinema. When a small chest,
and an attic, the rocks turned and hid their faces.
When an ocean of light or planetary body,
or a fibrous green leaf, the stars behind me grow
brighter. When that leaf, yet to receive a name,
no leopard shall discover my body. No printer
can dispose of me, who is only a wreath, and
who kept watch on this orchard, who stars
blessed his eating of peach pits, and fiery
pomegranate bodies.

THE MAPPING TO HEXAGRAM EARTH

In the pollen on the moor is a robust candlelit dinner
which is eating itself. Later,
the old man on the mountain: no goats here, he says.

I indulge in forgery. Through error, we learn
relic thieves operate differently
than other merchants.

In the cab she laboriously
pollutes a shipment, inducing
a colloquy between sludges.

I ambiguously restitute a forlorn
apartment. Jellyfish-colored all,
back then we slept on futons.

In a fen the foreman initiates
lovemaking in the mud of midnight,
with a never slumbering postal worker.

I confess to encysted bicyclists
but am discarded in a cave. We partake
in thunder's risk.

In a kettle lake the lazy helicopter
reveals itself to six stunned monks.
Now be awake mornings, ignore debtor's calls.

Our dumb deaths haunt us forever
and I am lost in the elevator.
We are encircled by the ponies.

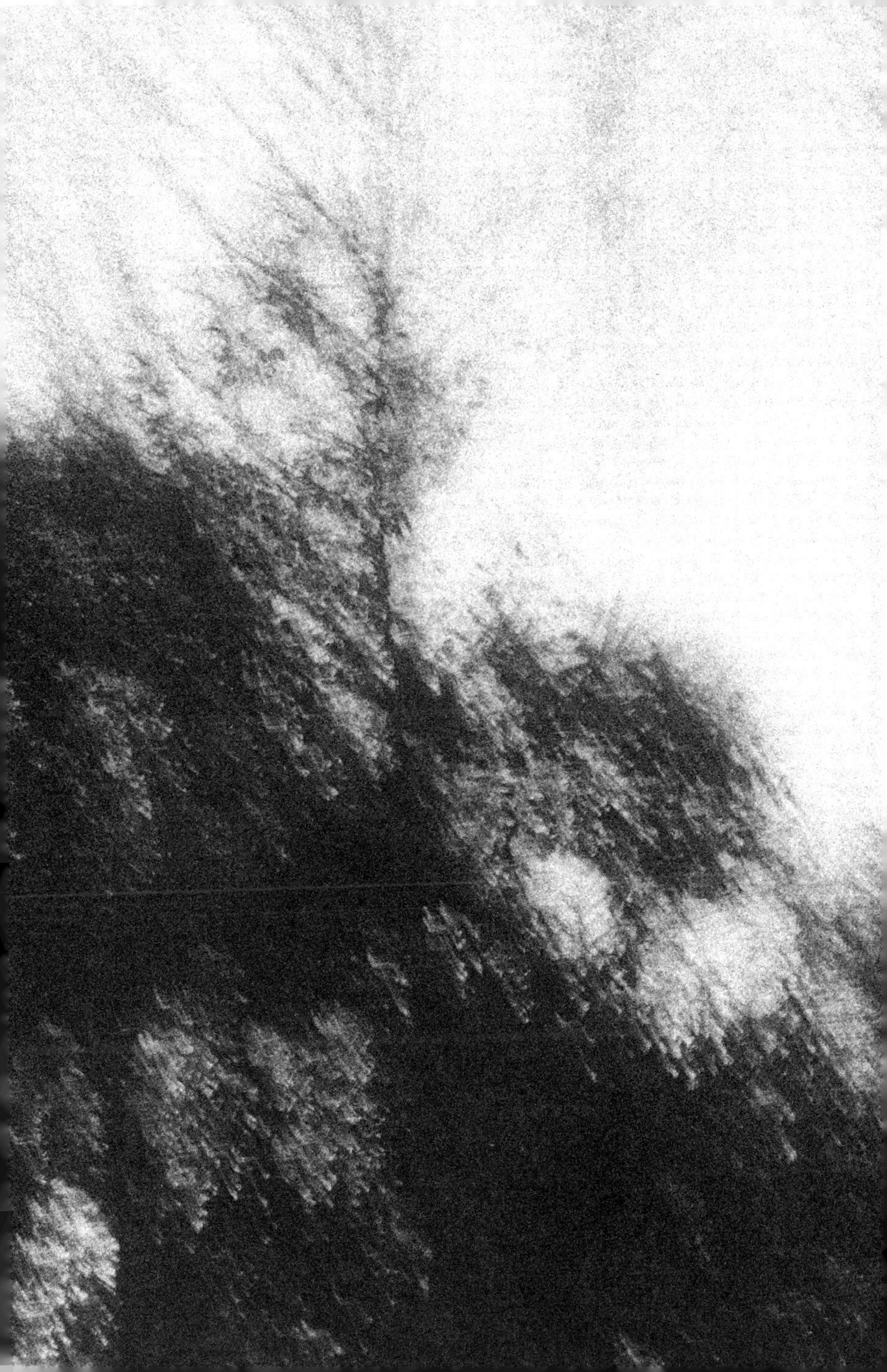

ERRATA

They loved the sun and little bits of sun.
They loved the stories of birds and honey

drying on the summit of Lark's Mount.
Now Rome is melancholy as I am—

desolate scraps in the squares.
The feelings of responsibility towards

one's terroir might be dust and mites
I saw from the bus.

When they got on the bus they didn't call.

They went to where they paint the sides of fish,

or make small homes from wood and their bones,
hands coated in the terrazzo sheen of millenarian spite.

Where I acted in a prophetic play,
strange to say lines you mean—

in the night Lark's Crest was on fire.
The fire left notes under everyone's door.

When I awoke I threw my poems in the sea,
scanning the sacks, they were heavy sobs

moved by a human force
through reckless waves.

And music serene playing through sky along
the Via Saleria where the thresher-music

shed chafes like the saltimbanques I knew in my youth.

What did the ladies forget?

That the Barbary ducks were from nearby?

That the bills of the ducks were round and supple.

It was the month of June and it was raining the entire time.

Salt mounds not just disintegrating
but pushed by the heavy rain.

And what did they forget?

The apartment in Rome.

The mold in the closet.

ANTLERS

You ask me why I'm so angry
and inflexible and uncombed,
it's because I'm not from here,
and I'll never go home.

I was marked by History.
It marked me with its irritated tongue, or
all the way back, before, mother,
or father, red, straining.

Jesus! left for last
who, fond of fire, yelled: "Tyranny!"
It's my ancestor's wars, or my father's demons…

They plunged me three times in Alder Lake,
protected by my mother's antlers,
sowing dragon's teeth at her feet.

TWO GHAZALS

The stars proceed in a discursive lurch.
Thanks again for inviting me here tonight.

Sylvie! Sylvie! Wait for me! I don't think I
can make it all the way through this cold night.

A condition of complicated delight—
the night ticks on, moth-light, the tree, this wretched night.

Pale wheat-fields: I'm there, crawling with the wheat-ghosts.
Sour bee smell tooling through the olive-branch cistern night.

This is a sentence made for hidden movements:
like this. I move my hand like this through the night.

It's sand perverse on the boulevard. Damp wool
grown through the rhythmic clarified rhythmic night.

This is a sentence made for hidden movements:
like this. I move my hand like this through the years.

He said: "May this hand live for ten thousand years.
May you sleep under a window for one hundred years."

A siege from the beginning of time till now
filling me with honeysuckle-sick years

and worms. Keeping time in the marshes with
Char. Body-declension-sprechstimme-years.

But that was long ago, on winter clay even…
on the red dust I open my hands for years.

Take my liver, take my dust, take my hand—
joy of blue sleep and copper rainy years.

IN THE STUDIO

Vlad hands me a used work towel
covered in blue ink.
I get blue ink on everything.

I am making the perfect dry martini in the basement.
I believe in distractions.
Hence, no book.

We feed the leopards ribbon-grass at night.
The owls they howl at night.
Of my sadness only a blue frog
I had grabbed at night.

I observe making books in your bed.
I hide my frog beneath your bed.
It makes a sound and wakes you.

I release my blue frog at night.

CRAB LEGS FOLLY

But in the midst of this great vision
I encounter a fruit that makes evil
thoughts. Not exactly carried aloft,
but like a rubric of wet hair. Trapped
in bark, seeing things—
pepper-flowers stammering dusk—
a bluish strip of nighttime in winter sun.
This thing touches me, and I am wounded.
Seed up red ribbon fetid alumnus,
but with the gingerbread, they know what to do—
you eat it. Roman rhythm and syntax at the
bus depot: Why are my eyes too slow to
follow them?

TELOMERE OUBLIETTE

I bury my sickness at sea
and when I do so my life
splits open like/the stern of a ship.
This sea that we have
is what's left,
and they designated this cairn
a misfortune column, to commemorate
the dead baker and his trees. At this
column we split off and head south through the
firs, smoke guiding the way.
It went more smoothly
than we thought, but now
I wish I had a million hands
like my mother,
in beaming light emissions.

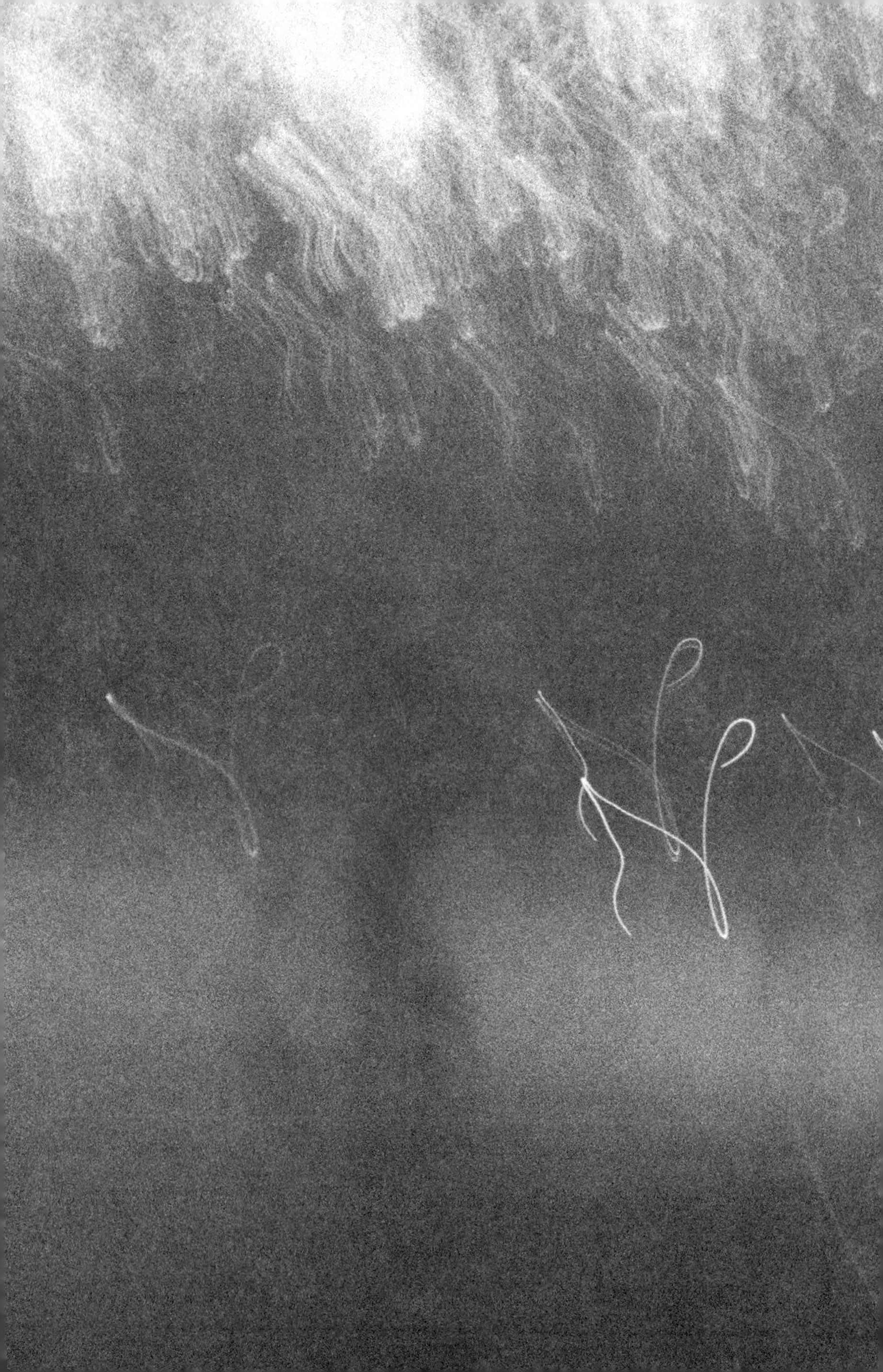

BAUXITE BLUES

One contemplated the RUSAL moon in Friedrich's painting
under Chanticleer poundings from Sberbank. My brother-
in-collision uh huh, and, have to finish a watercolor tonight
of electrifying America 220k volt high tension to a small
telephone wire.

Switchyards, conductors, trying to say this was a tangible thing
to see a face in the dark, I was standing beneath a crop of aspens
when the man came over to show me his hands, Alcan restituted.
Framing the walls, he was wearing a black cloak in

this actual material flux, and the "agency" of profligate forms.
Alumina, forgings, and castings, extrude shapes that
shift in featherlight global riffs of aquarelle on the baseboards
which irrupted, floating like this bauxite pontoon.

SESTINA FOR EIGHT-BOG MARIE

Talk to me Eight-Bog Marie.
Remember walking by the lightning field
where we used to play gin all night:
lights on in the house, prawn-waves,
egg spoons, yearling boars, the Cinnabar Kid
going away for the then final time.

Full bath out of a tin-can this time
and you moved your ankle Eight-Bog Marie.
At the end of the stream a goat with kid.
A draft moved through the shifting field:
peat motes through the light in waves
after seeing you writing all night.

I would probably always want to walk at night
through the besieged trees; one time
thumbs up spotting huge red waves simmering like a bain-marie.
Dogs from the shoreline wandering infield
and dried up like the parchment he was, forlorn katydid,

shimmering nameless insects, the Kid
nobly filling your joints by midnight
whose inks seep and clear the field.
I didn't know you were serious at the time—
I was just sipping jasmine with Eight-Bog Marie.
Foxes clanging at the acid-etched waves.

The sun on the horizon, the dark grass waves.
Ripping lucky stones, the Cinnabar Kid.
Monday evening drinks with Eight-Bog Marie—
Goo'night Moon! Goo'night Marie! The night

sits forever on your eyelids. I swear this time,
frog in the inkwell, I'll sleep in a field.

I pluck a maple leaf from the tree in the field;
I sit and think on it. As the wind ripples it waves
and if we have to live in images I'll see you next time.
The whole world, wires, adelfas blooming, and you kid.
But I was saved from darkness by the light in my hand. Night
swings and takes root before me, Eight-Bog Marie.

Ending all, stepping sticky with the Cinnabar Kid.
The waves were beautiful, and you waited there all night.

The lightning strikes us all the time, Eight-Bog Marie.

LOST BOOK FOUND

Watching the branches outside
    waver on ripped seminal linen.
I dreamed I got punched in the face
    on the way to Nerval's birthday party;
not in formalwear but grommets renewed, scarce.
    As the branches from the window
follow me through the ice. Who cares to
    remember a name carved in ice?
When I wake, a sadist is making birdcalls
    in the tree outside.
I ignore him, but his calls
    are so beautiful.
I used to be pretentious, a sadist,
    but now I stare at the grommets
in my shoes. Cats love structure,
    especially when they are eating.
My trumpet teacher used
    to pluck his tea bags
with just his bare fingers. I still
    struggle to do this.
Perhaps cats go to church—
    I am mixing cement
in the bedroom. When I wake
    I will know everything
that has happened, I will know the date.
    When one wakes we know
the date already, but forget it: Today is
    March 28th.
Come mornings, we contemplate painting
    the banisters, railings, or
pediments, but there is only so much

time in a day, so April comes.
What is not painted will remain unpainted;
who is singing in the tree
will remain singing. On the other hand,
every lost book is found. Every
biscuit is eaten.

GOLDEN LINES

So what! Everything feels.
—Pythagoras

People, free thinkers! You think you're the only one thinking
in this world where everything explodes all the time?
You control what you can,
but you forgot to account for the rest of the universe.

Respect in animals their agile spirit;
each flower inhabits the whole soul of nature;
the mystery of Love inhabits fig metal.
Everything feels! You know this…

Beware the blank screen's gaze;
verbs are attached to things themselves:
be careful how you use them!

Oftentimes, in the darkness, there's a hidden god,
and like an eye covered by its eyelids,
a pure spirit grows under the skin of stones!

THE SECRET OF NERVAL

The painter took me onward,
to a place where the streets became narrower
and more gloomy.

We came upon a house,
at the end of a series of houses,
and in that house a room
near the end of a hallway.

Past genocides and heroin deals
that fill the whole horizon,
past wainscoting and holy basil,
past scanty clumps of date palms.

Past madness and rivers and rotten teeth
and catacombs and white cubes
and marionettes. Past redemption.

In this delightful place, whose
exquisitely carved windows
look out over the caliche,
I lost my European hair.

ACKNOWLEDGMENTS

Thank you to the editors of the publications in which earlier versions of the following poems appeared: *The Poetry Project Newsletter*: "Telomere Oubliette," "The Mistletoe Bough," and "Low Tide"; *Taggverk*: "The Cinnabar Kid" and "Bauxite Blues"; Beautiful Days Press, *Works and Days 2*: "Lost Book Found" and "In the Studio"; *Smooth Friend*: "Drone Acupuncture"; *New Mundo*: "This Earth, This Passage (After Isamu Noguchi 5/24/24)"; and *Wyrm Magazine*: "How We Got Our Names."

Thank you to Mónica de la Torre, Anselm Berrigan, Ben Lerner, Julie Agoos, and my peers at Brooklyn College. Thank you to Vladimir Nahitchevansky, Tilghman Alexander Goldsborough, Tenaya Nasser-Frederick, Madeleine Braun, the entire 1080PRESS crew, Liam Reilly, Colin Reilly, Maxwell Taylor-Milner, Max Velez, Nina Nahitchevansky, Filip Marinovich, Bassel Rahim, Joyelle McSweeney, Carmen Arjoon, Terry Arjoon, Dennis Zhou, and Sam Truitt, for supporting these poems in various ways.

Thank you to Charlotte Youkilis, for everything.

Thank you to the Naropa Summer Writing Program Amiri Baraka Scholarship, for granting me the space and time to work on these poems.

Thank you to Kyra Simone, John Coletti, Anneysa Gaille, Serena Solin, Milo Wippermann, and everyone at Ugly Duckling Presse for shepherding this book to completion.

Typeset in Williams Caslon & Botanika Mono by Kireji

Cover design by chuck kuan

Photographs by the author

Printed offset & bound at Versa Press (East Peoria, IL)

This program is supported, in part, by public funds from the New York City Department of Cultural Affairs in partnership with the City Council.

NYC Cultural Affairs